carrot cake
& other favourites

THE AUSTRALIAN Women's Weekly

contents

Of all the cakes we eat, one of the most requested is the humble carrot cake! Perhaps that's because it's such a moist cake – always ready to eat and easy to keep; perhaps it's the combination of cake and frosting… perhaps it's just because it's a great cake! Whatever the reason, we have put together the classic carrot cake with some variations – and some of our other great favourites of all times – enjoy!

Pamela Clark

Food Director

classic carrot cake

prep + cook time 1 hour 35 minutes

1 cup (250ml) vegetable oil
1⅓ cups (250g) firmly packed brown sugar
3 eggs
3 cups (720g) firmly packed, coarsely grated carrot
1 cup (120g) coarsely chopped walnuts
2½ cups (375g) self-raising flour
½ teaspoon bicarbonate of soda
2 teaspoons mixed spice
lemon cream cheese frosting
30g butter
80g cream cheese, softened
1 teaspoon finely grated lemon rind
1½ cups (240g) icing sugar

1 Preheat oven to 160°C/160°C fan-assisted.
2 Grease deep 23cm-round cake tin, line base with baking parchment.
3 Beat oil, sugar and eggs in small bowl with electric mixer until thick and creamy. Transfer mixture to large bowl, stir in carrot and nuts, then sifted dry ingredients.
4 Pour mixture into prepared tin, bake cake about 1¼ hours. Cover loosely with foil halfway through cooking. Stand cake 5 minutes; turn onto wire rack to cool. Spread lemon cream cheese frosting over cold cake.
lemon cream cheese frosting Beat butter, cream cheese and rind in small bowl with electric mixer until light and fluffy; gradually beat in icing sugar.

serves 12
tip You will need about six medium carrots for this recipe.

carrot & orange cupcakes

prep + cook time 50 minutes

⅔ cup (160ml) vegetable oil
¾ cup (165g) firmly packed brown sugar
2 eggs
1 teaspoon finely grated orange rind
1½ cups (210g) firmly packed coarsely grated carrot
1¾ cups (260g) self-raising flour
¼ teaspoon bicarbonate of soda
1 teaspoon mixed spice
orange glacé icing
2 cups (320g) icing sugar
20g butter, melted
2 tablespoons orange juice, approximately

1 Preheat oven to 180°C/160°C fan-assisted. Line 12-hole
(⅓-cup/80ml) muffin pan with paper cases.
2 Beat oil, sugar, eggs and rind in small bowl with electric mixer
until thick and creamy. Transfer mixture to large bowl; stir in
carrot, then sifted dry ingredients.
3 Divide mixture into paper cases; bake about 30 minutes.
Stand cakes in pan 5 minutes before turning, top-side up, onto
wire rack to cool.
4 Meanwhile, make orange glacé icing. Spread cakes with icing.
orange glacé icing Sift icing sugar into small heatproof bowl; stir
in butter and enough juice to make a firm paste. Stir over small
saucepan of simmering water until spreadable.

makes 12
tip You need about two medium carrots (240g) for this recipe.

almond carrot cake

prep + cook time 1 hour 35 minutes

5 eggs, separated
1 teaspoon finely grated lemon rind
1¼ cups (275g) caster sugar
2 cups (480g) coarsely grated carrot
2 cups (240g) ground almonds
½ cup (75g) self-raising flour
2 tablespoons toasted slivered almonds
cream cheese frosting
100g cream cheese, softened
80g butter, softened
½ cup (80g) icing sugar
1 teaspoon lemon juice

1 Preheat oven to 180°C/160°C fan-assisted. Grease deep 19cm-square cake tin; line base with baking parchment.
2 Beat egg yolks, rind and sugar in small bowl with electric mixer until thick and creamy; transfer to large bowl. Stir in carrot, ground almonds and sifted flour.
3 Beat egg whites in small bowl with electric mixer until soft peaks form; fold into carrot mixture in two batches.
4 Pour mixture into tin; bake about 1¼ hours. Stand cake 5 minutes; turn, top-side up, onto wire rack to cool.
5 Meanwhile, make cream cheese frosting.
6 Spread cold cake with cream cheese frosting; sprinkle with slivered almonds.
cream cheese frosting Beat cream cheese and butter in small bowl with electric mixer until light and fluffy; gradually beat in icing sugar and juice.

serves 10

carrot & banana cake

prep + cook time 1 hour 35 minutes

1¼ cups (185g) plain flour
½ cup (75g) self-raising flour
1 teaspoon bicarbonate of soda
1 teaspoon mixed spice
½ teaspoon ground cinnamon
1 cup (200g) firmly packed brown sugar
¾ cup (90g) coarsely chopped walnuts or pecans
3 eggs, beaten lightly
2 cups finely grated carrot
1 cup mashed banana
1 cup (250ml) vegetable oil

1 Preheat oven to 160°C/140°C fan-assisted. Grease 24cm springform tin, line base with baking parchment.
2 Sift flours, soda, spices and sugar into large bowl, stir in remaining ingredients; pour cake mixture into prepared tin. Bake cake about 1¼ hours. Cool cake in tin.

serves 10
tip You will need about 4 medium carrots (480g) and 2 large over-ripe bananas (460g) for this recipe.

upside-down toffee banana cake

prep + cook time 1 hour 10 minutes

1 cup (220g) caster sugar
1 cup (250ml) water
2 medium bananas (400g), sliced thinly
2 eggs, beaten lightly
⅔ cup (160ml) vegetable oil
¾ cup (165g) firmly packed brown sugar
1 teaspoon vanilla extract
⅔ cup (100g) plain flour
⅓ cup (50g) wholemeal self-raising flour
2 teaspoons mixed spice
1 teaspoon bicarbonate of soda
1 cup mashed over-ripe banana

1 Preheat oven to 180°C/160°C fan-assisted. Grease deep 22cm-round cake tin; line base with baking parchment.
2 Stir caster sugar and the water in medium saucepan over heat, without boiling, until sugar dissolves; bring to a boil. Boil, uncovered, without stirring, about 10 minutes or until caramel in colour. Pour toffee into tin; top with sliced banana.
3 Combine egg, oil, brown sugar and extract in medium bowl. Stir in sifted dry ingredients, then mashed banana; pour mixture into tin. Bake, uncovered, about 40 minutes. Turn onto wire rack, peel off baking parchment. Serve cake warm or at room temperature with thick cream, if desired.

serves 8
tip You will need 2 large over-ripe bananas for this recipe.

top image: carrot & banana cake
bottom image: upside-down toffee banana cake

banana cake with passionfruit icing

ep + cook time 1 hour 25 minutes

25g butter, softened
cup (165g) firmly packed brown sugar
eggs
½ cups (225g) self-raising flour
teaspoon bicarbonate of soda
teaspoon mixed spice
cup mashed banana
cup (120g) soured cream
cup (60ml) milk

passionfruit icing
½ cups (240g) icing sugar
teaspoon soft butter
tablespoons passionfruit pulp, approximately

Preheat oven to 180°C/160°C fan-assisted. Grease 15cm x 25cm loaf tin; e base with baking parchment.

Beat butter and sugar in small bowl with electric mixer until light and ffy. Beat in eggs, one at a time, until combined.

Transfer mixture to large bowl; using wooden spoon, stir in sifted dry gredients, banana, cream and milk. Spread mixture into tin. Bake, covered, about 50 minutes. Stand cake 5 minutes then turn onto wire ck; turn cake top-side up to cool.

Make passionfruit icing.

Spread cold cake with passionfruit icing.

passionfruit icing Place icing sugar in small heatproof bowl; stir in butter d enough pulp to give a firm paste. Stir over hot water until icing is of a readable consistency, taking care not to overheat; use immediately.

rves 10
os You will need 2 large ripe bananas to make 1 cup of mashed banana. is important that the bananas are over-ripe: not only do they mash easily ut, if they are under-ripe, the cake will be too heavy.

apple cake

prep + cook time 1 hour 20 minutes

185g butter, chopped
2 teaspoons finely grated orange rind
⅔ cup (150g) caster sugar
3 eggs
1 cup (150g) self-raising flour
½ cup (75g) plain flour
⅓ cup (80ml) milk
2 medium apples (300g)
⅓ cup (90g) marmalade, warmed, strained

1 Preheat oven to 180°C/160°C fan-assisted. Grease deep 23cm-round cake tin; line base with baking parchment.
2 Beat butter, rind and sugar in medium bowl with electric mixer until light and fluffy. Beat in eggs, one at a time, until just combined. Sift about half of the flours over butter mixture, add about half of the milk; stir with a wooden spoon only until combined. Stir in remaining sifted flours and milk until mixture is smooth. Spread cake mixture evenly into prepared tin.
3 Peel, quarter and core apples. Make several closely placed cuts in the rounded side of each apple quarter, slicing about three-quarters of the way through each piece. Place quarters, rounded-side up, around edge of cake. Bake cake about 1 hour or until cooked when tested.
4 Stand cake 5 minutes before turning onto wire rack. Remove paper, turn cake right way up onto another rack. Brush warm marmalade over top of hot cake; cool before cutting.

serves 8

top image: raspberry & apple cakes; bottom image: apple cake

raspberry & apple cakes

prep + cook time 45 minutes

125g butter, softened
1 teaspoon vanilla extract
¾ cup (165g) caster sugar
2 eggs
1½ cups (225g) self-raising flour
½ cup (125ml) milk
150g fresh or frozen raspberries
1 large apple (200g), peeled, chopped finely
2 teaspoons icing sugar, sifted

Preheat oven to 180°C/160°C fan-assisted. Line 12-hole (⅓-cup/80ml) muffin pan with paper cases.

Beat butter, extract and sugar in small bowl with electric mixer until light and fluffy. Beat in eggs, one at a time. Stir in sifted flour and milk, in two batches. Stir in raspberries and apple.

Divide mixture into paper cases; bake about 30 minutes. Stand in pan 5 minutes before turning, top-side up, onto wire rack to cool. Dust with icing sugar.

makes 12

○ If using frozen raspberries, use straight from the freezer as thawed berries will bleed colour through the cake mix.

pear crumble cake

prep + cook time 1 hour 25 minutes

2 cups (500ml) water
1 cup (220g) caster sugar
2 cinnamon sticks
2 small (360g) pears, sliced thinly
125g butter
⅔ cup (150g) caster sugar, extra
2 eggs
1½ cups (225g) self-raising flour
crumble topping
½ cup (75g) plain flour
⅓ cup (75g) caster sugar
60g butter
½ cup (45g) desiccated coconut

1 Line base and side of 22cm springform tin with foil.
2 Combine the water, sugar and cinnamon in large frying pan; stir over heat, without boiling, until sugar dissolves. Add pears; simmer, uncovered, about 5 minutes or until just tender, drain on absorbent kitchen paper.
3 Preheat oven to 180°C/160°C fan-assisted.
4 Beat butter and extra sugar in small bowl with electric mixer until light and fluffy. Add eggs, one at a time, beating until just combined between additions. Add flour; beat on low speed until just combined, spread into prepared tin.
5 Top cake mixture with half the pears, sprinkle with half the crumble topping; repeat with remaining pears and topping. Bake cake 1 hour. Cool in tin.
crumble topping Blend or process ingredients until fine and crumbly.

serves 10
tip It is important to slice pears as thinly as possible. If the slices are too thick, the cake will sink in the centre.

plum & cinnamon cakes

prep + cook time 50 minutes

2 medium plums (200g)
185g butter, melted
1 cup (125g) ground almonds
6 egg whites, beaten lightly
1½ cups (240g) icing sugar
½ cup (75g) plain flour
1½ teaspoons ground cinnamon

1 Preheat oven to 200°C/180°C fan-assisted. Grease 12-hole (⅓-cup/80ml) muffin pan.
2 Halve plums; discard stones. Cut each half into three wedges. Place butter, ground almonds, egg whites, and sifted icing sugar, flour and cinnamon in medium bowl; stir until just combined. Divide mixture among pan holes. Place a plum wedge each cake.
3 Bake cakes about 25 minutes stand in pan 5 minutes. Turn ont wire rack to cool.

makes 12

upside down pear & pistachio cake

prep + cook time 50 minutes

¼ cup (35g) coarsely chopped unsalted pistachios
1 cup (220g) firmly packed brown sugar
1 large pear (330g), unpeeled, cored, sliced thinly
185g butter, softened
3 eggs
¼ cup (35g) plain flour
1¾ cups (210g) ground almonds

1 Preheat oven to 200°C/180°C fan-assisted. Grease shallow 22cm-round cake tin; line base with baking parchment.
2 Combine nuts and 2 tablespoons of the sugar in small bowl; sprinkle over base of tin, top with pear slices.
3 Beat butter and remaining sugar in small bowl with electric mixer until light and fluffy. Beat in eggs, one at a time. Stir in sifted flour and ground almonds.
4 Pour mixture into tin; bake about 35 minutes. Stand cake in tin 10 minutes before turning, top-side down, onto wire rack. Serve cake warm or cold.

serves 8
tip Unless a recipe instructs you to do otherwise, use roasted unsalted nuts when making a cake since the butter you use has probably already had salt added to it. Buy the freshest nuts you can: they should taste slightly sweet. And be sure to taste any nuts you've had around for a while before using them to make certain they haven't gone rancid.

top image: plum & cinnamon cakes;
bottom image: upside-down pear & pistachio cake

pistachio buttercake
with orange honey syrup

rep + cook time 1 hour 10 minutes

cups (280g) unsalted pistachios,
 chopped coarsely
35g butter, softened
 tablespoon finely grated
 orange rind
 cup (165g) caster sugar
 eggs
 cup (60ml) buttermilk
/2 cups (225g) self-raising flour
 cup (110g) plain flour

orange honey syrup
1 cup (220g) caster sugar
1 cup (250ml) water
1 tablespoon honey
1 cinnamon stick
1 teaspoon cardamom seeds
3 star anise
3 strips orange rind

Make orange honey syrup; cool.

Preheat oven to 180°C/160°C fan-assisted. Grease 23cm-square cake tin;
he base and sides with baking parchment, extending paper 2cm over the
des. Sprinkle nuts evenly over base of tin.

Beat butter, rind and sugar in small bowl with electric mixer until light
nd fluffy. Add eggs, one at a time, beating until just combined between
dditions; transfer mixture to large bowl. Stir in combined buttermilk and
 cup of the orange honey syrup, and sifted flours, in two batches.

Spread mixture into tin; bake about 40 minutes. Stand cake 5 minutes;
rn, top-side up, onto baking-parchment-covered wire rack. Brush surface
f hot cake with half of the remaining heated syrup.

Cut cake into squares, serve warm, drizzled with remaining heated syrup.

range honey syrup Stir ingredients in small saucepan over low heat,
ithout boiling, until sugar dissolves; bring to a boil. Remove from heat;
ool 15 minutes then strain.

erves 12

rhubarb custard tea cake

prep + cook time 1 hour 50 minutes (+ cooling)

200g butter, softened
½ cup (110g) caster sugar
2 eggs
1¼ cups (185g) self-raising flour
⅓ cup (40g) custard powder
4 fresh rhubarb stalks (300g), sliced lengthways
   then cut into 10cm lengths
20g butter, melted
2 teaspoons caster sugar, extra
custard
2 tablespoons custard powder
¼ cup (55g) caster sugar
1 cup (250ml) milk
20g butter
2 teaspoons vanilla extract

1 Make custard. Preheat oven to 180°C/160°C fan-assisted. Grease deep 20cm-round cake tin; line base with baking parchment.
2 Beat softened butter and sugar in small bowl with electric mixer until light and fluffy. Beat in eggs, one at a time. Transfer to medium bowl; stir in sifted flour and custard powder.
3 Spread half the mixture into tin; spread over custard. Dollop small spoonfuls of remaining cake mixture over custard; carefully spread with spatula to completely cover custard. Top cake mixture with rhubarb; brush gently with melted butter then sprinkle with extra sugar.
4 Bake cake about 1¼ hours; cool in tin.
custard Combine custard powder and sugar in small pan; gradually stir in milk. Cook, stirring, until mixture boils and thickens slightly. Remove from heat; stir in butter and extract. Press cling film over surface to prevent a skin forming; cool. Whisk until smooth before using.

serves 8

top image: rhubarb cake; **bottom image:** rhubarb custard tea cake

rhubarb cake

prep + cook time 1 hour
45 minutes

50g butter
1 teaspoon finely grated lemon
   rind
1½ cups (300g) firmly packed
   brown sugar
2 eggs
1 cup (150g) self-raising flour
1 cup (150g) plain flour
1 teaspoon ground cinnamon
1 cup (240g) soured cream
5 cups (500g) fresh rhubarb,
   trimmed, chopped coarsely
⅓ cup (75g) firmly packed
   brown sugar, extra
1 teaspoon ground cinnamon,
   extra

Preheat oven to 180°C/160°C
fan-assisted. Grease deep
23cm-round cake tin, line base
with baking parchment.
2 Beat butter, rind, sugar and
eggs in medium bowl with
electric mixer until light and fluffy.
Stir in sifted flours and cinnamon
and cream, in two batches; stir in
rhubarb. Spread into tin; sprinkle
with extra sugar and cinnamon.
3 Bake about 1½ hours. Stand
cake in tin 5 minutes; turn onto
wire rack to cool.

serves 10

ginger & lime dessert cake

prep + cook time 1 hour 30 minutes (+ refrigeration time)

250g butter, chopped
½ cup (110g) firmly packed dark
  brown sugar
⅔ cup (230g) golden syrup
12cm piece fresh ginger (60g),
  grated
¾ cup (180ml) whipping cream
2 eggs

1 cup (150g) plain flour
1 cup (150g) self-raising flour
½ teaspoon bicarbonate of soda
1 cup (50g) flaked coconut
lime syrup
½ cup (125ml) lime juice
½ cup (125ml) water
½ cup (110g) caster sugar

1 Preheat oven to 180°C/160°C fan-assisted. Grease deep 22cm-round cake tin; line base and side with baking parchment.
2 Melt butter in medium saucepan; add brown sugar, golden syrup and ginger. Stir over medium heat until sugar dissolves.
3 Whisk in cream, eggs and combined sifted flours and soda. Pour mixture into prepared tin; bake, uncovered, about 40 minutes.
4 Meanwhile, make lime syrup.
5 Pierce hot cake, still in tin, all over with skewer; drizzle hot lime syrup over cake. Cover; refrigerate about 3 hours or until cold.
6 Meanwhile, make mascarpone cream (see recipe opposite).
7 Remove cake from tin; line base and side of same cleaned tin with cling film. Split cake into three layers; return one layer of cake to prepared tin. Spread layer with 1 cup of the mascarpone cream; repeat with second cake layer and 1 cup of the remaining mascarpone cream, top with third cake layer. Cover; refrigerate 2 hours. Refrigerate remaining mascarpone cream, covered, until required.
8 Remove cake from tin, spread remaining mascarpone cream around side and top of cake; press coconut onto sides of cake.
lime syrup Stir ingredients in small saucepan over heat, without boiling, until sugar dissolves; bring to a boil. Reduce heat; simmer, uncovered, without stirring, 2 minutes. Strain into small heatproof jug.

serves 8
tip This cake is best made the day before required to allow for easy cutting. You will need about eight limes for this recipe.

ascarpone cream

hisk together 250g mascarpone cheese,
0ml whipping cream, 2 tablespoons icing
gar and 2 teaspoons finely grated lime
d in small bowl until soft peaks form.
efrigerate until required.

fresh ginger cake with golden ginger cream

prep + cook time 1 hour 15 minutes

250g butter, chopped
½ cup (110g) firmly packed brown sugar
⅔ cup (230g) golden syrup
12cm piece fresh ginger (60g), grated finely
1 cup (150g) plain flour
1 cup (150g) self-raising flour
½ teaspoon bicarbonate of soda
2 eggs, beaten lightly
¾ cup (180ml) whipping cream
golden ginger cream
300ml whipping cream
2 tablespoons golden syrup
2 teaspoons ground ginger

1 Preheat oven to 180°C/160°C fan-assisted. Grease deep 22cm-round cake tin.
2 Melt butter in medium saucepan; add sugar, syrup and ginger. Stir over low heat until sugar dissolves.
3 Whisk in combined sifted flours and soda then egg and cream. Pour mixture into tin; bake about 50 minutes. Stand cake 10 minutes; turn, top-side up, onto wire rack to cool.
4 Meanwhile, beat golden ginger cream ingredients in small bowl with electric mixer until soft peaks form. Serve cake with cream.

serves 8

iced gingerbread

prep + cook time 1 hour 15 minutes (+ cooling time)

1 cup (350g) golden syrup
1 cup (250ml) water
²/₃ cup (150g) firmly packed brown sugar
250g butter, chopped
3½ cups (525g) plain flour
1 teaspoon bicarbonate of soda
2 tablespoons ground ginger
1 teaspoon ground nutmeg
1 teaspoon ground cinnamon
lemon icing
60g butter, softened
2 teaspoons finely grated lemon rind
2 tablespoons lemon juice
2 cups (320g) icing sugar

1 Preheat oven to 160°C/140°C fan-assisted. Grease 23cm-square cake tin; line base with baking parchment, extending paper 5cm over sides.
2 Combine syrup, the water, sugar and butter in large saucepan; stir over low heat until smooth. Bring to a boil; remove from heat, cool to room temperature. Stir in sifted dry ingredients.
3 Pour mixture into tin; bake about 1 hour. Stand cake 5 minutes; turn, top-side up, onto wire rack to cool.
4 Meanwhile, make lemon icing. Spread cooled cake with icing.
lemon icing Beat butter and rind in small bowl until smooth; gradually stir in juice and sifted icing sugar.

serves 16

orange cake

prep + cook time 50 minutes

150g butter, softened
1 tablespoon finely grated
   orange rind
⅔ cup (150g) caster sugar
3 eggs
1½ cups (225g) self-raising flour
¼ cup (60ml) milk
¾ cup (120g) icing sugar
1½ tablespoons orange juice

1 Preheat oven to 180°C/160°C
fan-assisted. Grease deep
20cm-round cake tin.
2 Beat butter, rind, caster sugar,
eggs, flour and milk in medium
bowl with electric mixer at low
speed until just combined.
Increase speed to medium, beat
about 3 minutes or until mixture
is smooth.
3 Spread mixture into tin; bake
about 40 minutes. Stand cake
5 minutes; turn, top-side up, on
wire rack to cool.
4 Combine sifted icing sugar
and juice in small bowl; spread
over cake.

serves 12

lemon cake

ep + cook time 1 hour 20 minutes

25g butter, softened
teaspoons finely grated lemon rind
¼ cups (275g) caster sugar
eggs
½ cups (225g) self-raising flour
cup (125ml) milk
cup (60ml) lemon juice
mon mascarpone frosting
)0ml whipping cream
cup icing sugar
teaspoons finely grated lemon rind
50g mascarpone

Preheat oven to 180°C/160°C fan-assisted. Grease deep 20cm-round
ke tin; line base with baking parchment.
Make lemon mascarpone frosting. Refrigerate, covered, until required.
Beat butter, rind and sugar in small bowl with electric mixer until light
d fluffy. Add eggs, one at a time, beating until just combined between
dditions (mixture might separate at this stage, but will come together
ter); transfer mixture to large bowl. Stir in sifted flour, milk and juice, in
o batches.
Pour mixture into tin; bake about 50 minutes. Stand cake 5 minutes; turn,
p-side up, onto wire rack to cool.
Split cold cake into three layers, place one layer onto serving plate,
t-side up; spread with one-third of the frosting. Repeat layering process,
iishing with frosting.
mon mascarpone frosting Beat cream, sifted icing sugar and rind in small
owl with electric mixer until soft peaks form. Fold cream mixture into
ascarpone.

rves 12

p image: orange cake; **bottom image:** lemon cake

hummingbird cake

prep + cook time 1 hour 20 minutes

450g can crushed pineapple in syrup
1 cup (150g) plain flour
½ cup (75g) self-raising flour
½ teaspoon bicarbonate of soda
½ teaspoon ground cinnamon
½ teaspoon ground ginger
1 cup (200g) firmly packed brown sugar
½ cup (45g) desiccated coconut
1 cup mashed banana
2 eggs, beaten lightly
3/4 cup (180ml) vegetable oil
cream cheese frosting
60g cream cheese, softened
30g butter
1 teaspoon vanilla essence
1½ cups (240g) icing sugar

1 Preheat oven to 180°C/160° fan-assisted. Grease 23cm-square cake tin, line base with baking parchment.
2 Drain pineapple over medium bowl; reserve ¼ cup (60ml) syrup.
3 Sift flours, soda, spices and sugar into large bowl. Stir in pineapple, reserved syrup, coconut, banana, eggs and oil. Pour into prepared tin; bake about 50 minutes. Stand cake 5 minutes; turn onto wire rack to cool.
4 Spread cold cake with cream cheese frosting. Decorate cake with fresh flowers, if desired; remove flowers to serve.
cream cheese frosting Beat cream cheese, butter and essence in small bowl with electric mixer until light and fluffy; gradually beat in icing sugar.

serves 12
tip You will need about 2 large (460g) over-ripe bananas for this recipe.

pineapple cake with malibu cream

prep + cook time 1 hour 15 minutes

cup (75g) shredded coconut
50g can crushed pineapple
in syrup
25g butter, softened
cup (110g) caster sugar
eggs
½ cups (225g) self-raising flour

6 egg whites
½ cup (110g) caster sugar, extra
2 teaspoons icing sugar
malibu cream
300ml whipping cream
¼ cup (40g) icing sugar
1 tablespoon Malibu

Toast coconut in medium frying pan, stirring constantly, about 2 minutes or until browned lightly. Remove from pan; cool.

Drain pineapple over small bowl; reserve ½ cup of the syrup, discard remainder.

Preheat oven to 180°C/160°C fan-assisted. Grease two deep 20cm-round springform tins; line bases and sides with baking parchment.

Beat butter and sugar in small bowl with electric mixer until light and fluffy. Add eggs, one at a time, beating until just combined between additions. Transfer mixture to large bowl; stir in sifted flour, pineapple, then reserved syrup. Divide mixture between tins; bake 20 minutes.

Meanwhile, beat egg whites in small bowl with electric mixer until soft peaks form; gradually add extra caster sugar, beating until sugar dissolves between additions. Fold in toasted coconut.

Remove cakes from oven; working quickly; divide coconut mixture over cakes in tins, using spatula to spread evenly so tops are completely covered. Bake about 30 minutes. Stand cakes in tins 5 minutes; using small knife, carefully loosen meringue from baking parchment around inside of tin. Release sides of tins; cool.

Meanwhile, beat ingredients for malibu cream in small bowl with electric mixer until soft peaks form.

Place one cake on serving plate; spread with cream. Top with remaining cake; dust with sifted icing sugar.

serves 10

spice cake

prep + cook time 45 minutes

60g butter, softened
1 teaspoon vanilla extract
½ cup (110g) caster sugar
1 egg
1 cup (150g) self-raising flour
⅓ cup (80ml) milk
20g butter, melted, extra
spiced nuts
2 tablespoons shelled pistachios, chopped finely
2 tablespoons blanched almonds, chopped finely
2 tablespoons pine nuts, chopped finely
¼ cup (40g) icing sugar
½ teaspoon ground allspice
½ teaspoon ground cardamom
1 teaspoon ground cinnamon

1 Preheat oven to 180°C/160°C fan-assisted. Grease 20cm-round cake tin.
2 Beat butter, extract, sugar and egg in small bowl with electric mixer until light and fluffy. Stir in sifted flour and milk.
3 Spread mixture into tin; bake about 25 minutes. Stand cake 5 minutes; turn, top-side up, onto wire rack to cool.
4 Meanwhile, make spiced nuts.
5 Brush cooled cake with extra butter; sprinkle with spiced nuts. Serve cake warm.
spiced nuts Place nuts in strainer; rinse under cold water. Combine wet nuts in large bowl with icing sugar and spices; spread mixture onto oven tray, toast in moderate oven about 10 minutes or until nuts are dry.

serves 12

orange poppyseed syrup cake

prep + cook time 1 hour 15 minutes

⅓ cup (50g) poppyseeds
¼ cup (60ml) milk
185g butter, chopped
1 tablespoon finely grated orange rind
1 cup (220g) caster sugar
3 eggs
1½ cups (225g) self-raising flour
½ cup (75g) plain flour
½ cup (60g) ground almonds
½ cup (125ml) orange juice
orange syrup
1 cup (220g) caster sugar
⅔ cup (160ml) orange juice
⅓ cup (80ml) water

1 Grease deep 23cm-round cake tin, line base and side with baking parchment. Combine seeds and milk in small bowl, stand 20 minutes. Preheat oven to 180°C/160°C fan-assisted.
2 Beat butter, rind and sugar in small bowl with electric mixer until light and fluffy; beat in eggs one at a time, beat until combined. Transfer mixture to large bowl, stir in sifted flours, ground almonds, juice and poppyseed mixture.
3 Spread into prepared tin; bake about 55 minutes. Stand cake 5 minutes. Turn cake onto wire rack over tray, pour hot orange syrup over hot cake. Pour any syrup in tray into jug, pour back over cake.
orange syrup Combine ingredients in small saucepan, stir over heat, without boiling, until sugar is dissolved. Simmer, uncovered, without stirring, 2 minutes.

serves 16

madeira cake

prep + cook time 1 hour
15 minutes

180g butter, softened
2 teaspoons finely grated lemon
   rind
⅔ cup (150g) caster sugar
3 eggs
¾ cup (110g) plain flour
¾ cup (110g) self-raising flour
⅓ cup (55g) mixed peel
¼ cup (35g) slivered almonds

1 Preheat oven to 160°C/140°C
fan-assisted. Grease deep
20cm-round cake tin; line base
with baking parchment.
2 Beat butter, rind and sugar in
small bowl with electric mixer
until light and fluffy; beat in eggs,
one at a time. Transfer mixture to
large bowl, stir in sifted flours.
3 Spread mixture into tin; bake
30 minutes. Remove cake from
oven; sprinkle with peel and nuts.
Return to oven; bake about
30 minutes. Stand cake for
5 minutes; turn, top-side up,
onto wire rack to cool.

serves 12

top image: orange poppyseed syrup
cake; **bottom image:** madeira cake

coconut cake

prep + cook time 1 hour 5 minutes

125g butter, softened
½ teaspoon coconut essence
1 cup (220g) caster sugar
2 eggs
½ cup (40g) desiccated coconut
1½ cups (225g) self-raising flour
1¼ cups (300g) soured cream
⅓ cup (80ml) milk
coconut ice frosting
2 cups (320g) icing sugar
1⅓ cups (100g) desiccated coconut
2 egg whites, beaten lightly
pink food colouring

1 Preheat oven to 180°C/160°C fan-assisted. Grease deep
23cm-square cake tin; line with baking parchment.
2 Beat butter, essence and sugar in small bowl with electric mixer until
light and fluffy. Beat in eggs, one at a time. Transfer mixture to large
bowl; stir in coconut, sifted flour, sour cream and milk, in two batches.
3 Spread mixture into tin; bake about 40 minutes. Stand cake
5 minutes; turn, top-side up, onto wire rack to cool.
4 Meanwhile, make coconut ice frosting. Drop alternate spoonfuls of
white and pink frosting onto cake; marble over top of cake.
coconut ice frosting Sift icing sugar into medium bowl; stir in coconut
and egg white. Place half the mixture in small bowl; tint with pink
colouring.

serves 20

chocolate coconut cakes

prep + cook time 1 hour

6 eggs
⅔ cup (150g) caster sugar
⅓ cup (50g) cornflour
½ cup (75g) plain flour
⅓ cup (50g) self-raising flour
2 cups (160g) desiccated coconut
chocolate icing
4 cups (640g) icing sugar
½ cup (50g) cocoa powder
15g butter, melted
1 cup (250ml) milk

1 Preheat oven to 180°C/160°C fan-assisted. Grease 20cm x 30cm baking tin; line with baking parchment, extending paper 5cm over long sides.
2 Beat eggs in large bowl with electric mixer about 10 minutes or until thick and creamy; gradually beat in sugar, dissolving between additions. Fold in triple-sifted flours.
3 Spread mixture into tin; bake about 35 minutes. Turn cake immediately onto a baking-parchment-covered wire rack to cool.
4 Meanwhile, make icing. Cut cake into 16 pieces; dip each square in icing, drain off excess. Toss squares in coconut. Place cakes onto wire rack to set.
chocolate icing Sift icing sugar and cocoa into medium heatproof bowl; stir in butter and milk. Set bowl over medium saucepan of simmering water; stir until icing is of a coating consistency.

makes 16

pink jelly coconut cakes Make 80g packet of strawberry jelly as per instructions; refrigerate until set to consistency of unbeaten egg white. Dip cake squares into jelly then desiccated coconut. Beat 300ml whipping cream until firm peaks form. Halve cakes horizontally; sandwich cakes with whipped cream.

mocha coconut cakes Add 1 tablespoon cocoa powder to dry ingredients for cake; fold into egg mixture. Combine 1 tablespoon instant coffee granules with 1 tablespoon boiling water; fold into cake mixture then follow recipe instructions from step 3. Beat 300ml whipping cream with 2 tablespoons coffee-flavoured liqueur until firm peaks form. Once icing has set, halve cakes horizontally then sandwich with whipped cream.

dark chocolate mud cake

prep + cook time 3 hours (+ cooling time)

675g dark eating chocolate, chopped
400g unsalted butter, chopped
1½ tablespoons instant coffee granules
1¼ cups (310ml) water
1¼ cups (275g) firmly packed brown sugar
1¾ cups (260g) plain flour
½ cup (75g) self-raising flour
4 eggs
⅓ cup (80ml) coffee-flavoured liqueur
dark chocolate ganache
½ cup (125ml) double cream
400g dark eating chocolate, chopped

1 Preheat oven to 160°C/140°C fan-assisted. Grease deep
19cm-square cake tin; line with baking parchment.
2 Combine chocolate, butter, coffee, the water and sugar in large
saucepan; stir over low heat until smooth. Cool 15 minutes.
3 Whisk in sifted flours, eggs and liqueur. Pour mixture into tin; bake
about 2½ hours. Cool cake in tin.
4 Meanwhile, make dark chocolate ganache.
5 Turn cake, top-side up, onto plate; spread with ganache. Top with
raspberries, if desired.
dark chocolate ganache Bring cream to a boil in small saucepan;
remove from heat, add chocolate, stir until smooth. Refrigerate, stirring
occasionally, about 30 minutes or until spreadable.

serves 16

white choc mud cake

prep + cook time 2 hours 30 minutes

180g white chocolate, chopped
350g unsalted butter, chopped
2⅔ cups (590g) caster sugar
1½ cups (375ml) milk
2 cups (300g) plain flour
⅔ cup (100g) self-raising flour
1 teaspoon vanilla extract
3 eggs
1 quantity white chocolate
 ganache (see recipe opposite)

1 Preheat oven to 160°C/140°C fan-assisted. Grease deep 22cm-round cake tin; line with baking parchment.
2 Combine chocolate, butter, sugar and milk in large saucepan stir over low heat until smooth. Pour mixture into large bowl; cool 15 minutes.
3 Whisk in sifted flours, extract and eggs. Pour mixture into tin; bake about 2 hours. Cool cake in tin.
4 Turn cake, top-side up, onto plate; spread with ganache (see recipe, opposite).

serves 12

caramel mud cake

prep + cook time 2 hours (+ cooling time)

185g butter, chopped
150g white eating chocolate, chopped coarsely
1 cup (200g) firmly packed brown sugar
⅓ cup (80ml) golden syrup
1 cup (250ml) milk
1½ cups (225g) plain flour
½ cup (75g) self-raising flour
2 eggs
white chocolate ganache
½ cup (125ml) double cream
300g white chocolate, chopped coarsely

1   Preheat oven to 160°C/140°C fan-assisted. Grease deep 23cm-round cake tin; line base and side with baking parchment.
2   Combine butter, chocolate, sugar, golden syrup and milk in medium saucepan; stir over low heat, without boiling, until smooth. Transfer mixture to large bowl; cool 15 minutes.
3   Whisk in sifted flours, then eggs, one at a time. Pour mixture into prepared tin; bake about 1½ hours. Stand cake in tin 30 minutes; turn onto wire rack to cool. Spread top and side with white chocolate ganache.
white chocolate ganache   Bring cream to boil in small saucepan; pour over chocolate in small bowl, stirring until chocolate melts. Cover; refrigerate, stirring occasionally, about 30 minutes or until spreadable.

serves 12

top image: white choc mud cake; **bottom image:** caramel mud cake

marbled chocolate mud cake

prep + cook time 1 hour 25 minutes

250g butter, softened
1 teaspoon vanilla extract
1¼ cups (275g) caster sugar
3 eggs
2¼ cups (335g) self-raising flour
¾ cup (180ml) buttermilk
¼ cup (25g) cocoa powder
¼ cup (60ml) milk

95g white chocolate chips
95g dark chocolate chips
chocolate butter cream
125g butter, softened
1½ cups (240g) icing sugar
2 tablespoons milk
2 tablespoons cocoa powder

1 Preheat oven to 180°C/160°C fan-assisted. Grease deep 22cm-round cake tin; line base with baking parchment.
2 Beat butter, extract and sugar in small bowl with electric mixer until light and fluffy. Add eggs, one at a time, beating until just combined between additions; transfer mixture to large bowl. Stir in sifted flour and buttermilk, in two batches.
3 Divide cake mixture between two bowls. Blend sifted cocoa with milk; stir into one of the bowls of mixture with white chocolate chips. Stir dark chocolate chips into remaining mixture.
4 Drop alternate spoonfuls of mixtures into tin, then pull skewer back and forth through cake mixture several times to achieve a marbled effect. Bake cake about 1 hour. Stand cake 5 minutes; turn, top-side up, onto wire rack to cool.
5 Meanwhile, make chocolate butter cream.
6 Drop alternate spoonfuls of the two butter cream mixtures onto cake; spread over top and side of cake.
chocolate butter cream Beat butter in small bowl with electric mixer until light and fluffy. Gradually beat in half of the icing sugar, then the milk, then the remaining icing sugar. Transfer half of the mixture to another small bowl; stir sifted cocoa into one of the bowls.

serves 10

classic sponge cake

prep + cook time 40 minutes

4 eggs
¾ cup (165g) caster sugar
⅔ cup (100g) cornflour
¼ cup (30g) custard powder
1 teaspoon cream of tartar
½ teaspoon bicarbonate of soda
300ml whipping cream
1 tablespoon icing sugar
½ teaspoon vanilla extract
¼ cup (80g) strawberry jam, warmed
250g strawberries, sliced thinly

1   Preheat oven to 180°C/160°C fan-assisted. Grease and flour two deep 22cm-round cake tins.
2   Beat eggs and caster sugar in small bowl with electric mixer about 5 minutes or until thick and creamy; transfer to large bowl.
3   Sift dry ingredients twice onto paper, sift over egg mixture; fold ingredients together.
4   Divide mixture evenly between tins. Bake, uncovered, about 20 minutes. Turn sponges immediately onto baking-parchment-lined wire rack; turn sponges top-side up to cool.
5   Beat cream, icing sugar and extract in small bowl with electric mixer until firm peaks form. Place one sponge on serving plate; spread with jam, then cream mixture. Top with strawberries, then remaining sponge. Dust with sifted icing sugar, if desired.

serves 10

brown sugar sponge

prep + cook time 50 minutes (+ cooling time)

eggs
¾ cup (165g) firmly packed dark brown sugar
cup (150g) cornflour
teaspoon cream of tartar
½ teaspoon bicarbonate of soda
00ml whipping cream

praline
⅓ cup (75g) granulated sugar
¼ cup (60ml) water
½ teaspoon malt vinegar
⅓ cup (45g) roasted hazelnuts

Preheat oven to 180°C/160°C fan-assisted) Grease two deep 22cm-round
ake tins.
Beat eggs and brown sugar in small bowl with electric mixer about
0 minutes or until thick and creamy; transfer to large bowl.
Sift cornflour, cream of tartar and bicarbonate of soda twice onto baking
archment then sift over egg mixture; gently fold dry ingredients into egg
ixture. Divide mixture between tins; bake about 18 minutes. Turn sponges
mmediately onto baking-parchment-covered wire racks to cool.
Meanwhile, make praline.
Beat cream in small bowl with electric mixer until firm peaks form; fold in
raline. Place one sponge on serving plate; spread with half of the cream
ixture. Top with remaining sponge; spread with remaining cream mixture.

raline Stir sugar, the water and vinegar in small saucepan over heat,
ithout boiling, until sugar dissolves; bring to a boil. Reduce heat; simmer,
ncovered, without stirring, about 10 minutes or until syrup is golden
rown. Add hazelnuts; pour praline mixture onto baking-parchment-
overed tray. Cool about 15 minutes or until set. Break praline into pieces
en blend or process until mixture is as fine (or coarse) as desired.

erves 10

sacher torte

prep + cook time 1 hour 45 minutes (+ cooling time)

100g dark chocolate, chopped coarsely
1 cup (250ml) water
125g butter, chopped
1¼ cups (250g) firmly packed brown sugar
3 eggs
1 cup (150g) self-raising flour
¼ cup (25g) cocoa powder
½ cup (60g) ground almonds
⅓ cup (110g) apricot jam
dark chocolate ganache
200g dark eating chocolate, chopped coarsely
⅔ cup (160ml) double cream

1 Preheat oven to 160°C/140°C fan-assisted. Grease deep 23cm-round cake tin, line base with baking parchment.
2 Combine chocolate and the water in small saucepan, stir over low heat until chocolate is melted; cool.
3 Beat butter and sugar in small bowl with electric mixer until combined; beat in eggs, one at a time, beating well between additions. Transfer mixture to large bowl, stir in sifted flour and cocoa, ground almonds and chocolate mixture.
4 Pour mixture into prepared tin. Bake about 1 hour and 10 minutes. Stand cake 10 minutes; turn onto wire rack to cool.
5 Split cold cake in half; sandwich with jam. Place cake on wire rack over tray. Spread cake all over with a thin layer of ganache.
6 Heat remaining ganache over hot water until pourable (do not overheat) Strain ganache, pour over cake; working quickly, smooth top and side of cake. Allow ganache to set at room temperature.
dark chocolate ganache Place chocolate and cream in small heatproof bow over saucepan of simmering water, stir until chocolate is melted.

serves 12

chocolate & pecan torte

prep + cook time 1 hour 20 minutes (+ standing and refrigeration time)

200g dark eating chocolate, chopped coarsely
150g butter, chopped
5 eggs, separated
¾ cup (165g) caster sugar
1½ cups (150g) ground pecans (see tip)
dark chocolate ganache
½ cup (125ml) double cream
200g dark eating chocolate, chopped coarsely

1 Preheat oven to 180°C/160°C fan-assisted. Grease deep 22cm-round cake tin; line base and side with baking parchment.
2 Stir chocolate and butter in small saucepan over low heat until smooth; cool 10 minutes.
3 Beat egg yolks and sugar in small bowl with electric mixer until thick and creamy. Transfer to large bowl; fold in chocolate mixture and ground pecans.
4 Beat egg whites in small bowl with electric mixer until soft peaks form; fold into chocolate mixture, in two batches. Pour mixture into tin; bake about 55 minutes. Stand cake 15 minutes; turn, top-side up, onto baking-parchment-covered wire rack to cool.
5 Meanwhile, make dark chocolate ganache.
6 Pour ganache over cake; refrigerate cake 30 minutes before serving.
dark chocolate ganache Bring cream to a boil in small saucepan. Remove from heat; add chocolate, stir until smooth.

serves 12
tip If you can't find ground pecans, simply blend or process 150g of roasted pecans until they are finely ground. Be sure to use the pulse button, however, because you want to achieve a flour-like texture, not a paste.

black forest torte

prep + cook time 1 hour 15 minutes (+ refrigeration time)

370g packet rich chocolate cake mix (see tip)
60g butter
2 eggs
⅓ cup (80ml) buttermilk
½ cup (120g) soured cream
60g dark chocolate, melted
¼ cup (60ml) Kirsch
900ml whipping cream
cherry filling
2 x 425g cans pitted black cherries
1½ tablespoons cornflour

1 Preheat oven to 180°C/160°C fan-assisted. Grease deep 23cm-round cake tin, line base with baking parchment.
2 Beat cake mix, butter, eggs, buttermilk, soured cream and cooled chocolate in small bowl with electric mixer on low speed until combined. Beat on medium speed 2 minutes or until mixture changes to a lighter colour.
3 Spread cake mixture into prepared tin; bake about 50 minutes. Stand cake in tin 5 minutes; turn onto wire rack to cool.
4 Split cold cake horizontally into three layers; place one layer on serving plate, brush with some of the liqueur. Spread cake layer with half the cold cherry filling and a quarter of the whipped cream; top with a second layer. Repeat layering with remaining liqueur, filling and another quarter of the whipped cream, finishing with the third cake layer. Decorate cake with remaining half of whipped cream; refrigerate 3 hours.
cherry filling Drain cherries over jug, reserve ⅔ cup (160ml) syrup. Chop cherries roughly. Combine blended cornflour and syrup with cherries in small saucepan; stir over heat until mixture boils and thickens; cover, cool.

serves 10
tip We used a packet cake mix that does not call for butter to be added; you do not need to use the ingredients listed on the packet.

raspberry brownie ice-cream cake

prep + cook time 1 hour (+ freezing)

1 litre vanilla ice-cream, softened
150g frozen raspberries
125g butter, chopped coarsely
200g dark eating chocolate, chopped coarsely
½ cup (110g) caster sugar
2 eggs
1¼ cups (185g) plain flour
150g milk eating chocolate, chopped coarsely
1 tablespoon icing sugar

1 Line deep 23cm-round cake tin with cling film, extending film so it will cover tin. Combine ice-cream and raspberries in medium bowl. Spoon ice-cream into tin; smooth surface. Fold cling film over to enclose. Freeze 3 hours or until firm.
2 Preheat oven to 160°C/140°C fan-assisted. Remove ice-cream from tin, still wrapped in cling film; place on tray. Return to freezer.
3 Grease same tin; line base and side with baking parchment.
4 Combine butter, dark chocolate and sugar in medium saucepan; stir over low heat until smooth. Cool 10 minutes.
5 Stir in eggs, sifted flour and milk chocolate. Spread mixture into tin. Bake brownie about 30 minutes; cool in tin.
6 Split brownie in half. Sandwich ice-cream cake between brownie slices; serve immediately, dusted with sifted icing sugar. Serve with fresh raspberries, if you like.

serves 12

choc espresso gateau

prep + cook time 1 hour 10 minutes

1 tablespoon instant coffee
    granules
2 tablespoons boiling water
370g packet chocolate cake mix
2 eggs
20g soft butter
¾ cup (180ml) water
300ml whipping cream
100g dark chocolate, grated

1 Preheat oven to 180°C/160°C fan-assisted. Grease and line deep 20cm-round cake tin.
2 Dissolve coffee granules in boiling water; cool.
3 Combine cake mix, eggs, butter, water and coffee mixture in medium bowl. Beat on low speed with electric mixer until combined. Increase speed to medium; beat 3 minutes.
4 Pour mixture into tin; bake about 45 minutes. Stand cake in tin 10 minutes before turning, top-side up, onto wire rack to cool. Split cake into three. Beat cream until firm peaks form; stir in grated chocolate. Sandwich cake layers with chocolate cream.

serves 12

classic chocolate cake

prep + cook time 1 hour 10 minutes (+ cooling time)

125g butter, softened
1 teaspoon vanilla extract
1¼ cups (275g) caster sugar
2 eggs
1⅓ cups (200g) self-raising flour
½ cup (50g) cocoa powder
⅔ cup (160ml) water
chocolate icing
90g dark eating chocolate, chopped coarsely
30g butter
1 cup (160g) icing sugar
2 tablespoons hot water

1 Preheat oven to 180°C/160°C fan-assisted. Grease deep
20cm-round cake tin; line with baking parchment.
2 Beat butter, extract, sugar, eggs, sifted flour and cocoa, and
the water in large bowl with electric mixer on low speed until
ingredients are combined. Increase speed to medium; beat
about 3 minutes or until mixture is smooth and paler in colour.
3 Spread mixture into tin; bake about 1 hour. Stand cake
5 minutes; turn, top-side up, onto wire rack to cool.
4 Meanwhile, make chocolate icing. Spread cake with icing.
chocolate icing Melt chocolate and butter in small heatproof
bowl over small saucepan of simmering water; gradually stir
in sifted icing sugar and the hot water, stirring until icing is
spreadable.

serves 20

top image: choc espresso gateau;
bottom image: classic chocolate cake

chocolate banana cake

prep + cook time 1 hour 40 minutes

⅔ cup (160ml) milk
2 teaspoons lemon juice
150g butter, softened
1 cup (220g) caster sugar
2 eggs
2 cups (300g) self-raising flour
½ teaspoon bicarbonate of soda
1 cup mashed banana
100g dark eating chocolate, grated finely
creamy choc frosting
200g dark eating chocolate
1 cup (160g) icing sugar
½ cup (120g) soured cream

1 Preheat oven to 170°C/150°C fan-assisted. Grease deep 22cm-round cake tin; line base with baking parchment.
2 Combine milk and juice in small jug; stand 10 minutes.
3 Meanwhile, beat butter and sugar in small bowl with electric mixer until light and fluffy. Beat in eggs, one at a time, until just combined; transfer mixture to large bowl. Stir in sifted flour and bicarbonate of soda, banana, milk mixture and chocolate.
4 Spread mixture into tin; bake about 1 hour 10 minutes. Stand cake 5 minutes; turn, top-side up, onto wire rack to cool.
5 Meanwhile, make creamy choc frosting; spread cold cake with frosting.
creamy choc frosting Melt chocolate in medium heatproof bowl over medium saucepan of simmering water; gradually stir in icing sugar and soured cream.

serves 10

baked lemon ricotta cheesecake

prep + cook time 1 hour 50 minutes (+ cooling time)

1 cup (100g) digestive biscuit crumbs
½ cup (60g) ground almonds
80g butter, melted
filling
2½ cups (500g) ricotta cheese, sieved
1 cup (250g) mascarpone cheese
⅔ cup (150g) caster sugar
1 tablespoon finely grated lemon rind
¼ teaspoon ground cinnamon
3 eggs
⅓ cup (55g) sultanas

1 Grease 22cm springform tin, line base and side with baking parchment.
2 Combine crumbs, ground almonds and butter in medium bowl. Press mixture over base of prepared tin, refrigerate until firm.
3 Preheat oven to 160°/140° fan-assisted.
4 Pour filling over base, place tin on oven tray. Bake cheesecake about 1½ hours or until filling is just firm in centre. Turn oven off, cool in oven with door ajar. Cover; refrigerate cheesecake overnight.
filling Beat cheeses, sugar, rind and cinnamon in medium bowl with electric mixer until smooth. Add eggs, beat until just combined. Stir in sultanas.

serves 10

top image: baked lemon ricotta cheesecake;
bottom image: new york cheesecake

new york cheesecake

prep + cook time 1 hour
25 minutes (+ cooling time)

250g digestive biscuits
125g butter, melted
750g cream cheese
3 eggs
cup (220g) caster sugar
¾ cup (180g) soured cream
2 teaspoons finely grated lemon
rind
¼ cup (60ml) lemon juice

Line base of 22cm springform
tin with foil. Process biscuits until
finely crushed, add butter;
process until combined.

Press biscuit mixture over base
and side of prepared tin. Place
on oven tray; chill 30 minutes.

Preheat oven to 160°/140°
fan-assisted.

Beat the remaining ingredients
in medium bowl with electric
mixer until smooth. Pour cheese
mixture into biscuit crust. Bake
cheesecake about 1 hour or until
just set in centre. Turn oven off,
cool in oven with door ajar.
Cover; refrigerate cheesecake
overnight. Serve with fresh figs
if desired.

serves 12

dundee cake

prep + cook time 3 hours 30 minutes

2 cups (300g) currants
2 cups (340g) raisins, chopped coarsely
3 cups (500g) sultanas
½ cup (125ml) dark rum
150g butter
1 cup (200g) firmly packed brown sugar
4 eggs
½ cup (125ml) strawberry jam
1 cup (210g) glacé cherries, chopped coarsely
2 cups (340g) mixed peel
1 cup (140g) slivered almonds
2 cups (300g) plain flour
½ cup (75g) self-raising flour
½ teaspoon ground cinnamon
½ teaspoon ground allspice
blanched almonds and extra glacé cherries, to decorate
¼ cup (60ml) dark rum, extra

1 Combine dried fruit and rum in large bowl, cover; stand overnight.
2 Preheat oven to 150°C/130°C fan-assisted. Grease deep 23cm-round cake tin, line base and side with three layers baking parchment, extending paper 5cm above edge of tin.
3 Beat butter and sugar in small bowl with electric mixer until combined. Add eggs, one at a time, beating until just combined between additions; stir in jam. Stir into fruit mixture, then stir in cherries, peel, slivered almonds and sifted dry ingredients.
4 Spread cake mixture into prepared tin; decorate top with blanched almonds and extra glacé cherries, if desired. Bake cake about 3 hours. Brush top of hot cake with extra rum, cover tightly with foil; cool in tin.

serves 36

fruit & nut cake

prep + cook time 2 hours 5 minutes (+ standing time)

½ cup (115g) coarsely chopped
    glacé pineapple
½ cup (125g) coarsely chopped
    glacé apricots
1½ cups (250g) pitted dried dates
½ cup (110g) red glacé cherries
½ cup (110g) green glacé cherries
1 cup (170g) brazil nuts
½ cup (75g) macadamia nuts
2 eggs
½ cup (110g) firmly packed brown
    sugar
1 tablespoon dark rum
100g butter, melted

⅓ cup (50g) plain flour
¼ cup (35g) self-raising flour
fruit & nut topping
⅓ cup (75g) coarsely chopped
    glacé pineapple
¼ cup (55g) red glacé cherries,
    halved
¼ cup (55g) green glacé cherries,
    halved
¼ cup (40g) brazil nuts
¼ cup (35g) macadamia nuts
toffee topping
½ cup (110g) caster sugar
¼ cup (60ml) water

1   Preheat oven to 150°C/130°C fan-assisted. Grease 20cm-ring cake tin;
line base and side with baking parchment, extending it 5cm above side.
2   Combine fruit and nuts in large bowl.
3   Beat eggs and sugar in small bowl with electric mixer until thick. Add
rum, butter and sifted flours; beat until just combined. Stir egg mixture
into fruit mixture. Press mixture firmly into prepared tin.
4   Make fruit and nut topping. Gently press topping evenly over cake
mixture; bake, covered, 1 hour. Uncover; bake further 45 minutes. Stand
cake in tin 10 minutes.
5   Meanwhile, make toffee topping. Turn cake, top-side up, onto wire
rack; drizzle with toffee topping.
fruit & nut topping   Combine ingredients in medium bowl.
toffee topping   Combine ingredients in small saucepan, stir over heat
without boiling until sugar dissolves; bring to a boil. Reduce heat; simmer,
uncovered, without stirring, about 10 minutes or until mixture is golden.
Remove from heat; stand until bubbles subside before using.

serves 20

3 cups (500g) sultanas
1½ cups (250g) mixed peel
¾ cup (120g) coarsely chopped
 raisins
¾ cup (120g) coarsely chopped
 pitted dried dates
⅔ cup (140g) coarsely chopped
 pitted prunes
½ cup (125g) coarsely chopped
 glacé apricots
⅔ cup (150g) coarsely chopped
 glacé pineapple
½ cup (70g) slivered almonds
½ cup (60g) coarsely chopped
 walnuts
1 tablespoon finely grated
 orange rind
½ cup (110g) caster sugar
¼ cup (60ml) orange juice
½ cup (125ml) Grand Marnier
250g butter, softened
½ cup (110g) firmly packed
 brown sugar
5 eggs
2 cups (300g) plain flour
2 tablespoons Grand Marnier,
 extra
1kg ready-made fondant icing
1 egg white, beaten lightly
½ cup (80g) icing sugar, sifted
to finish
25cm-round covered cake board
decorative ribbon
13g packet silver cachous

1   Use spatula and tiny pieces of fondant
to patch holes on top and side of cake.
2   Using rolling pin dusted with icing
sugar, carefully lift fondant onto the cake.

grand marnier fruit cake

prep + cook time 5 hours 40 minutes (+ standing and cooling time)

Combine fruit, nuts and rind in large bowl. Cook caster sugar in large frying pan over low heat, without stirring, until it begins to melt then stir until sugar is melted and browned lightly. Remove from heat, slowly stir in juice; return to low heat, stir until toffee dissolves (do not boil). Add liqueur; pour over fruit mixture, cover tightly with cling film. Store mixture in cool, dark place for 10 days, stirring every day.

Preheat oven to 150°C/130°C fan-assisted. Line base and sides of deep 22cm-round or cake tin with one thickness of brown paper and two thicknesses of baking parchment, extending papers 5cm above edge.

Beat butter and brown sugar in small bowl with electric mixer until just combined; beat in eggs, one at a time, until just combined between additions. Stir butter mixture into fruit mixture, mix in flour; spread mixture into prepared tin. Tap tin firmly on bench to settle mixture into tin; level cake mixture with wet spatula.

Bake cake, uncovered, for 3½ hours. Remove from oven, brush with extra liqueur; cover hot cake with foil then turn upside down to cool overnight.

Trim top of cake with sharp knife to ensure it sits flat when turned upside down. Mix a little fondant and cold boiled water to a sticky paste. Spread tablespoons of paste into the centre of a sheet of baking parchment about 5cm larger than the cake; position cake upside down on paper.

Using spatula and small pieces of fondant, patch any holes on cake.

Brush egg white evenly over cake. Knead fondant on surface dusted with icing sugar until smooth; roll to 7mm thickness. Lift fondant onto cake with rolling pin, smoothing fondant all over cake with hands dusted with icing sugar. Using sharp knife, cut excess fondant away from base of cake.

Mix scraps of fondant and cold boiled water to a sticky paste. Spread about 2 tablespoons of paste in centre of board; centre cake on board. Using sharp craft knife or scalpel, carefully cut away excess baking parchment extending around base of cake.

Secure ribbon around cake using pins (remove to a safe place before cutting cake). Push cachous gently into fondant in the design of your choice.

serves 30

brandied light fruit cake

prep + cook time 2 hours 50 minutes

1¼ cups (185g) plain flour
1¼ cups (185g) self-raising flour
185g butter, chopped coarsely
4 cups (750g) mixed dried fruit
¾ cup (165g) raw sugar
¾ cup (180ml) hot milk
2 tablespoons brandy
2 eggs, beaten lightly

1 Preheat oven to 150°C/130°C fan-assisted. Grease deep 20cm-round cake tin, line base and side with three layers baking parchment, extending paper 5cm above edge of tin.
2 Combine flours in large bowl, rub in butter, then stir in the remaining ingredients.
3 Spread cake mixture into prepared tin; bake cake about 2½ hours. Cover hot cake tightly with foil; cool in tin.

serves 30

top image: boiled fruit cake;
bottom image: brandied light fruit ca

boiled fruit cake

prep + cook time 3 hours 15 minutes

2⅓ cups (375g) sultanas
2¼ cups (375g) chopped raisins
¾ cup (110g) currants
½ cup (105g) glacé cherries, halved
250g butter, chopped coarsely
1 cup (200g) firmly packed brown sugar
½ cup (125ml) sweet sherry
¼ cup (60ml) water
1 tablespoon treacle
2 teaspoons finely grated orange rind
2 teaspoons finely lemon rind
5 eggs, beaten lightly
1¾ cups (260g) plain flour
⅓ cup (50g) self-raising flour
extra glacé cherries, to decorate

1 Combine fruit, butter, sugar, sherry and the water in large saucepan. Stir over heat, without boiling, until butter melts and sugar dissolves. Bring to a boil, then remove from heat. Transfer mixture to large heatproof bowl; cool.
2 Preheat oven to 150°C/130°C fan-assisted. Grease deep 19cm-square cake tin or deep 23cm-round cake tin, line base and sides with three layers baking parchment, extending paper 5cm above edge of tin.
3 Stir treacle, rinds and egg into fruit mixture, then stir in flours. Spread cake mixture into prepared tin; decorate top with extra glacé cherries, if desired. Bake cake about 2¾ hours. Cover hot cake tightly with foil; cool in tin.

serves 36

glossary

allspice also known as pimento or Jamaican pepper; available whole or ground.

almonds

blanched skins removed.

ground also known as almond meal; nuts are powdered to a coarse flour texture.

slivered cut lengthways.

bicarbonate of soda also called baking soda.

brazil nuts native to South America, a triangular-shelled oily nut with an unusually tender white flesh and a mild, rich flavour. Good for eating as well as cooking, the nuts can be eaten raw or cooked, or can be ground into flour for baking.

buttermilk fresh low-fat milk cultured to give a slightly sour, tangy taste; low-fat yogurt or milk can be substituted.

cardamom can be bought in pod, seed or ground form. Has a distinctive, aromatic, sweetly rich flavour.

chocolate

chips hold their shape in baking.

dark eating made of cocoa liquor, cocoa butter and sugar.

milk eating most popular eating chocolate, mild and very sweet; similar in make-up to dark, but with the addition of milk solids.

white eating contains no cocoa solids, deriving its sweet flavour from cocoa butter. Is very sensitive to heat.

cinnamon dried inner bark of the shoots of the cinnamon tree. Available as a stick or ground.

cocoa powder also known as unsweetened cocoa; cocoa beans that have been fermented, roasted, shelled, ground into powder then cleared of most of the fat content.

coconut

desiccated unsweetened and concentrated, dried finely shredded.

flaked dried flaked coconut flesh.

shredded thin strips of dried coconut.

coffee-flavoured liqueur we use either Kahlua or Tia Maria coffee-flavoured liqueur.

cornflour also known as cornstarch; used as a thickening agent in cooking.

cream of tartar the acid ingredient in baking powder; added to confectionery mixtures to help prevent sugar from crystallising. Keeps frostings creamy and improves volume when beating egg whites.

cream we used fresh cream in this book, unless otherwise stated. Also known as pure cream and pouring cream; has no additives unlike commercially thickened cream. Minimum fat content 35%.

soured a thick commercially-cultured soured cream. Minimum fat content 35%.

whipping a cream that contains a thickener. Has a minimum fat content of 35 per cent.

cream cheese a soft cow's-milk cheese with a fat content ranging from 14 per cent to 33 per cent.

custard powder instant mixture used to make pouring custard; similar to North American instant pudding mixes.

date fruit of the date palm tree; eaten fresh or dried, on their own or in prepared dishes. About 4cm to 6cm in length, oval and plump, thin-skinned, with a honey-sweet flavour and sticky texture.

essences synthetically produced substances used in small amounts to impart their respective flavour to foods. An extract is made by actually extracting the flavour from a food product. In the case of vanilla, pods are soaked, usually in alcohol, to capture the authentic flavour. Both extracts and essences will keep indefinitely if stored in a cool dark place.

flour

plain all-purpose flour.

self-raising plain flour sifted with baking powder (a raising agent consisting mainly of 2 parts cream of tartar to 1 part bicarbonate of soda) in the proportion of 150g flour to 2 level teaspoons baking powder.

ginger, fresh also called green or root ginger, it is the thick

narled root of a tropical plant.
an be kept, peeled, covered
th dry sherry in a jar and
frigerated, or frozen in an
tight container.
acé fruit fruit such as cherries,
eaches, pineapple, orange and
cron cooked in heavy sugar
rup then dried.

olden syrup a by-product of
fined sugarcane; pure maple
rup or honey can be
bstituted.
and marnier a brandy-based
ange-flavoured liqueur.
rsch cherry-flavoured liqueur.
acadamias native to Australia,
rich and buttery nut; store in
frigerator because of its high
content.

alibu a coconut-flavoured rum.
ixed peel candied citrus peel.
ixed spice a blend of ground
ices usually consisting of
nnamon, allspice and nutmeg
ied nut of an evergreen tree;
ailable in ground form or you
n grate your own with a fine
ater.

passionfruit also known as
granadilla; a small tropical fruit,
native to Brazil, comprised of a
tough dark-purple skin
surrounding edible black
sweet-sour seeds.

pecans Native to the United
States; golden-brown, buttery
and rich. Good in savoury and
sweet dishes; especially good in
salads.

pine nuts also known as pignoli;
small, cream-coloured kernels
obtained from the cones of
different varieties of pine trees.
pistachios pale green, delicately
flavoured nut inside hard
off-white shells. To peel, soak
shelled nuts in boiling water
about 5 minutes; drain, then pat
dry.
poppy seeds small, dried,
bluish-grey seeds of the poppy
plant. Poppy seeds have a
crunchy texture and a nutty
flavour. Available whole or
ground in most supermarkets.
ready-made fondant icing also
called soft icing, ready-to-roll
and prepared fondant.

ricotta a soft, sweet, moist,
white, cow's-milk cheese with a
low fat content (about 8.5 per
cent) and a slightly grainy texture.
The name roughly translates as
'cooked again' and refers to
ricotta's manufacture from a whey
that is itself a by-product of other
cheese making.
rum, dark we prefer to use an
underproof rum (not overproof)
for a more subtle flavour.
star anise a dried star-shaped
pod, the seeds of which taste of
aniseed.
sugar
brown an extremely soft, fine
granulated sugar retaining
molasses for its deep colour
and flavour.
caster also known as superfine
or finely granulated table sugar.
dark brown an extremely soft,
fine-grained sugar retaining the
deep flavour and colour of
molasses.
icing also known as confectioners'
sugar or powdered sugar.
raw natural brown granulated
sugar.
treacle thick, dark syrup not
unlike molasses; a by-product of
sugar refining.
vanilla essence obtained from
vanilla beans infused in alcohol
and water.
vanilla extract obtained from
vanilla beans infused in water; a
non-alcoholic version of essence.
vegetable oil Any number of
oils sourced from plants rather
than animal fats.
vinegar, malt made from
fermented malt and beech
shavings.

77

conversion charts

MEASURES

The cup and spoon measurements used in this book are metric: one measuring cup holds approximately 250ml; one metric tablespoon holds 20ml; one metric teaspoon holds 5ml.

All cup and spoon measurements are level.

The most accurate way of measuring dry ingredients is to weigh them. When measuring liquids, use a clear glass or plastic jug with metric markings.

We use large eggs with an average weight of 60g.

WARNING This book may contain recipes for dishes made with raw or lightly cooked eggs. These should be avoided by vulnerable people such as pregnant and nursing mothers, invalids, the elderly, babies and young children.

DRY MEASURES

METRIC	IMPERIAL
15g	½oz
30g	1oz
60g	2oz
90g	3oz
125g	4oz (¼lb)
155g	5oz
185g	6oz
220g	7oz
250g	8oz (½lb)
280g	9oz
315g	10oz
345g	11oz
375g	12oz (¾lb)
410g	13oz
440g	14oz
470g	15oz
500g	16oz (1lb)
750g	24oz (1½lb)
1kg	32oz (2lb)

LIQUID MEASURES

METRIC	IMPERI
30ml	1 fl
60ml	2 fl
100ml	3 fl
125ml	4 fl
150ml	5 fl oz (¼ pint/1 g
190ml	6 fl
250ml	8 fl
300ml	10 fl oz (½ pi
500ml	16 fl
600ml	20 fl oz (1 pi
1000ml (1 litre)	1¾ pir

LENGTH MEASURES

METRIC	IMPERI
3mm	⅛
6mm	¼
1cm	½
2cm	¾
2.5cm	1
5cm	2
6cm	2½
8cm	3
10cm	4
13cm	5
15cm	6
18cm	7
20cm	8
23cm	9
25cm	10
28cm	11
30cm	12in (1

OVEN TEMPERATURES

These oven temperatures are only a guide for conventional ovens. For fan-assisted ovens, check the manufacturer's manual.

	°C (CELSIUS)	°F (FAHRENHEIT)	GAS MARK
Very low	120	250	½
Low	150	275–300	1–2
Moderately low	160	325	3
Moderate	180	350–375	4–5
Moderately hot	200	400	6
Hot	220	425–450	7–8
Very hot	240	475	9

Reprinted in 2011 by Octopus
Publishing Group Limited based on
materials licensed to it by ACP
Magazines Ltd, a division of PBL Med
Pty Limited
54 Park St, Sydney
GPO Box 4088, Sydney, NSW 2001
phone (02) 9282 8618;
fax (02) 9267 9438
acpbooks@acpmagazines.com.au;
www.acpbooks.com.au

OCTOPUS BOOKS
Design: Chris Bell
Food Director: Pamela Clark

Published and Distributed in the
United Kingdom by Octopus Publishir
Group Limited
Endeavour House
189 Shaftesbury Avenue
London WC2H 8JY
United Kingdom
phone + 44 (0) 207 632 5400;
fax + 44 (0) 207 632 5405
aww@octopusbooks.co.uk;
www.octopusbooks.co.uk
www.australian-womens-weekly.com

Printed and bound in China

International foreign language rights,
Brian Cearnes, ACP Books
bcearnes@acpmagazines.com.au

To order books:
telephone LBS on 01903 828 503
order online at
www.australian-womens-weekly.com
or www.octopusbooks.co.uk